This notebook belongs to:

*'I never dreamed about success. I worked for it.'*
ESTÉE LAUDER

*'It's not that I'm so smart, it's just that I stay with problems longer.'*
ALBERT EINSTEIN

*'I work hard because I love my work.'*
BILL GATES

*'Without labour nothing prospers.'*

SOPHOCLES

*'Do not hurry; do not rest.'*
JOHANN WOLFGANG VON GOETHE

# Dynamo

# Dynamo Mantra:
## *Plan for the Future*

Dynamos tend to be more *planful*
and *self-disciplined* than other personality
types – they have a *clear vision* for the
future and a *strategy* for *how to get there*.

# Personality Profile

*Organised ∗ Driven ∗ Visionary*
*Resourceful ∗ Focused*

Dynamos are achievers – they like to set themselves clear goals and take on personal projects, and they always have a clear plan. Planning is second nature to a Dynamo. Whether it's writing a shopping list or creating a two-week travel itinerary, Dynamos like to have their lives mapped out. They are the friend who has thrown multiple surprise parties and has all their contacts' birthdays calendarised. A Dynamo's attention to detail means they give their best to whatever they put their mind to but they can also tend toward perfectionism, especially in a work context. In their professional lives, Dynamos like to work in teams and on projects that are structured and have clear tasks and deadlines. They prefer an environment with a clear hierarchical structure in which roles are clearly marked out without ambiguity.

Dynamos live a life of routine, and it pays off. They have a set of activities that they pursue with focus and dedication. Whatever a Dynamo puts their mind to, they find a way to accomplish. Whether that's short-term goals, such as increasing their running pace, or long-term goals, like getting a job promotion, Dynamos are unwavering in their focus and drive. They plan and strategise tirelessly – and make sure they stick to their schedule.

Dynamos' orderliness manifests in all aspects of their life – they have a specific Spotify playlist for concentration, for working out and for socialising. If Dynamos take risks, such as taking a new job or moving to a new location, the risks are always calculated and well-researched, which means they're less likely to make mistakes. A lack of control and being pushed out of their comfort zone makes Dynamos feel uneasy.

Dynamos are often guided by logic over emotion. They are adept at keeping their emotions in check and are less comfortable expressing how they feel outside of close relationships. They like to be pragmatic and take a practical approach to matters in life. When it comes to values, Dynamos are more likely to follow the tried and tested rather than something completely new.

# The Big Five Personality Traits

*The 'Big Five' model was developed by psychologists in the field of personality science as a framework to describe human personality. The five broad traits outlined are: openness to experience, conscientiousness, extraversion, agreeableness and neuroticism – or 'OCEAN' for short.*

Personality researchers have found that those who score highest in the trait of **OPENNESS TO EXPERIENCE** tend to be 'cognitive explorers' – deep thinkers who like to interrogate their own perceptions and emotions, and who are curious and investigative about ideas and philosophical arguments. While Dynamos can be intellectually curious compared to other personality types, they prefer to follow a well-trodden path. Dynamos value experiences but are less likely to do something just for experience's sake. Instead, they prefer to build towards tangible goals and will engage in an activity if it leads to something. A Dynamo is likely to have a set of activities that they pursue with single-minded passion and focus, almost always leading to achieving a goal.

Of all the personality types, Dynamos score highest on the spectrum of **CONSCIENTIOUSNESS.** Conscientiousness refers to the tendency to be responsible, organised and hard-working. Those who are most conscientious will exhibit more goal-oriented behaviour, meaning that when they make a plan or set a long-term goal, they usually stick to it. They also model good self-regulation and impulse control. Dynamos are big Marie Kondo fans – they enjoy the fruits of an afternoon spring cleaning or decanting their toiletries into travel-sized bottles before a trip away. Dynamos are also known to binge watch interior-design programmes!

The quality of **EXTRAVERSION** refers to an individual's social energy and the conditions they need in order to recharge. In general, extraverts gain energy through interactions with people while introverts have less social energy, or require particular social conditions, and recharge by spending time alone. It's important to remember that introversion is not to be confused with shyness – introverts can be as sociable and people-loving as extraverts, they just need less stimulation and prefer smaller groups.

Introvert Dynamos often keep a journal and may own an impressive array of stationery. They enjoy robust one-to-one relationships and usually have a close group of friends, of whom they are the designated organiser. Extravert Dynamos take calculated risks, for instance: they may love adventurous travel but will have done all the research beforehand; if they decide to go hiking, they will have saved all the routes on their phone (and printed them out!) before they go. You can identify an extravert Dynamo as the host of a party because they are the one making sure everyone's glass is full and the food is doing the rounds.

**AGREEABLENESS** refers to an individual's preference for altruism and social harmony. Perceived to be friendly, optimistic and affectionate, highly agreeable individuals are less 'me' and more 'we', and they may have a hard time saying no to others or going against the grain. Dynamos can fall anywhere on the spectrum of agreeableness but introvert Dynamos tend to score more highly than other personality types. Introvert Dynamos can prefer to underplay their accomplishments out of consideration for others rather than taking credit when it is due.

**NEUROTICISM** is associated with sensitivity to emotions, self-criticism and general anxiety. Those who score highly in neuroticism tend to experience negative emotions more strongly than other personality types and, therefore, can be less even-tempered. High levels of neuroticism can also result in a more cynical outlook on life and being less comfortable in one's own skin. Again, Dynamos can fall anywhere on the spectrum of neuroticism. However, as they are often perfectionists, they may experience a rise in anxiety and preoccupying thoughts when it comes to completing a task.

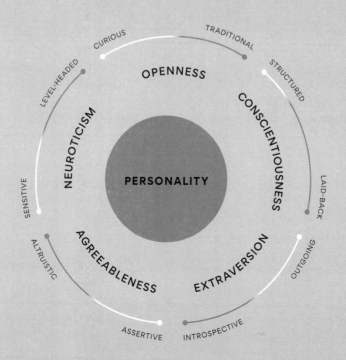

# Super Powers

## DISCIPLINE

Dynamos' commitment is unwavering. They won't start a task or project unless they can see it through (Dynamos make great long-distance runners!). When sitting down to a task, a Dynamo won't stop until it's done (even if it means losing sleep in the process). This sense of discipline is an asset across many parts of a Dynamo's life, whether they apply it to learning to rock climb or successfully completing a two-year project.

## TIME MANAGEMENT

Time management is a Dynamo's strong suit. Dynamos thrive on having their life organised and are skilled at identifying and prioritising tasks by urgency and importance. Dynamos like to give each task their full attention and put in the effort until it reaches the required standard before moving onto something else. More than any other personality type, when a deadline is looming, Dynamos can swing into action and focus on the end goal. However, Dynamos are not immune to distraction and would do well to turn off their phone notifications while they work.

## TAKING RESPONSIBILITY

Dynamos have a strong sense of duty and responsibility. On holiday, it is likely that a Dynamo will have made the bookings, checked the weather forecast and informed their friends, reminding them to pack appropriate clothing. A Dynamo will never forget a birthday or find themselves short of a baking ingredient mid-recipe. This isn't to say that a Dynamo won't let loose, just that they take pride in being responsible and organised.

## CALM

As Dynamos are analytical and driven more by logic than emotions, they are often calmer during times of stress and conflict than other personality types. A Dynamo will tend to hold off on an emotional reaction until they have engaged with a situation rationally. When making an important decision, such as a career move or embarking on a new relationship, a Dynamo will write a pros and cons list and bounce their ideas off close friends and family, and only then make an informed choice. Their calm nature and practical skill set make Dynamos excellent leaders, able to chart a course in times of unexpected stress.

'Think like a queen.
A queen is not
afraid to fail.
Failure is another
stepping-stone
to greatness.'

*

OPRAH WINFREY

## PATIENCE

Slow and steady wins the race for Dynamos. Dynamos are realistic about how long things take and allow themselves time to work at something until they are happy with it, so they are naturally patient with others. Whether teaching a parent how to use Zoom or shopping around for the perfect dress for a friend's wedding, Dynamos exhibit much more patience than other personality types. Their even-tempered, and at times stoic, nature makes them great in a crisis.

# Growth Areas

### DEALING WITH THE ABSTRACT

While Dynamos are even-tempered, they can struggle to adapt to a situation in which they don't feel in control. When things don't go to plan, Dynamos may find it difficult to switch gears and go with the flow. As a Dynamo, recognise that this starts with mindset. First, try to accept that you can't control everything. Then, try to focus your energy on things you can influence and let go of whatever is beyond your control.

### BUILDING RESILIENCE

As Dynamos are such high achievers, they might struggle when they meet failure. Whether missing out on a job or missing the last train home, Dynamos can find it difficult to see the big picture when things don't go to plan. Flexibility is an essential part of resilience. Next time your plans are disrupted, try to see it as an opportunity to adapt and change course. While your default response may be to feel dejected, see flexibility as a skill that you can build over time. By learning how to be more resilient in the small things, you'll be better equipped to respond in all situations.

### RESISTING JUDGEMENT

As Dynamos are organised and attached to specific ways of doing things, they can occasionally display a 'holier than thou' attitude when encountering a different approach. For example, as Dynamos are goal-oriented and pragmatic, they are less likely to respect those who appear more laid-back and unstructured. Dynamos may also be irked by those who don't take as much interest in facts. As a Dynamo, if you find yourself becoming judgemental, try to notice what triggered that reaction. Before reaching a conclusion about someone, stop and consider where they are coming from.

## REDUCING THE NEED FOR PERFECTIONISM

As high achievers who like to see things through to the end, Dynamos often set unattainably high standards for themselves and others. A Dynamo will feel the pressure to cross every 't' and dot every 'i'. At work, a Dynamo may end up taking on other people's workload just to ensure that it is done to a standard they are happy with. This can quickly lead to a tipping point where they are working at 1 am, don't have the time to get everything done and delay other priorities, creating a bottleneck.

Overcoming perfectionism is tricky but it is something that can be developed over time. Start by assessing your standards. Are they too high? Do you often find that you and others can't meet them? If so, start to set more realistic goals and challenge yourself to stick to them without going above and beyond.

## EXPRESSING FEELINGS

As Dynamos use logic to guide their decisions, this can sometimes lead them to internalise and repress emotions. Dynamos may suppress a 'negative' emotion such as anger, when research overwhelmingly indicates that channelling this emotion in the right way can help reduce stress and increase optimism. As a Dynamo, if you feel yourself getting angry, don't jump to suppress it. Acknowledge your feelings. Then ask yourself which elements of the situation are within your control and what you can do to improve it. Remember that expressing emotions is not the problem, it's how you manage them.

## 5 Things a Dynamo Will Say

'Wait until it's perfect'

'You'll get there in the end'

'It's worth the effort'

'Slow and steady wins the race'

'Don't forget!'

'Productivity
is being able to
do things that you
were never able
to do before.'

✳

FRANZ KAFKA

# Life Hacks

### GET UP AT THE SAME TIME EVERY DAY

Dynamos welcome routine. When a Dynamo starts the day in the way they expect, they feel a sense of control that trickles into the rest of the day. On weekdays, try to go to sleep and get up at the same time to gain a sense of mastery and control.

### SET MICRO-GOALS

Dynamos like to work towards goals as it gives them a sense of accomplishment. But they don't need to be big milestones or a New Year's resolution – as a Dynamo, try setting yourself micro-goals to increase the frequency of feeling that joyous sense of achievement. For instance, if you run, decide on a certain number of kilometres to complete in a month and reward yourself each time you do a run towards that. If you have a list of films and books you want watch and read this year, enjoy the satisfaction of crossing each off as you go.

### MAKE LISTS

Lists are gratifying for a Dynamo. They allow a Dynamo to plan their workload, as well as giving that sense of satisfaction when things are crossed off. Psychological research suggests that list-making has multiple benefits, from reducing stress and clarifying thoughts to freeing up important cognitive resources to encourage focus on things that matter. If you've embraced list-making, try working with an app to make it more of an automatic habit.

## 5 Things a Dynamo Should Have in Their Wallet

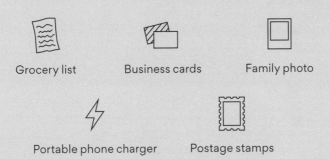

Grocery list    Business cards    Family photo

Portable phone charger    Postage stamps

## USE YOUR SUNDAY

A Dynamo likes nothing more than being ready and prepared to start work on a Monday. To begin the week feeling organised and in control, set aside part of your Sunday to prepare. If you like to cook, do your meal prep and grocery shopping for the week. To ensure you wake refreshed and ready to go, try to engage in some low-energy activities before you sleep, such as yoga or watching a film, so you get a good night's rest.

## UNWIND YOUR MIND

For every personality type, it's important to find a pursuit that calms your mind. Dynamos use routine as a means of reducing stress levels. As a Dynamo, make a list of familiar activities that bring you calm: it could be making your favourite comfort food for dinner, listening to that Spotify playlist that always brightens your mood or meeting a friend who never fails to tell you stories that entertain you and make you forget your woes.

# Compatibility

## WHO DO YOU CONNECT WITH?

As Dynamos value dependability and loyalty, they tend to connect most with those who mirror these values. Dynamos are drawn to those who are trustworthy, who make plans and, most importantly, stick to them. A Dynamo will have friends from different parts of their life – such as colleagues, friends from a social-football team or people they met at university – but they tend to connect most with those they've known for a long time, with whom they've shared deep and meaningful experiences and with whom they have gone through the ups and downs of life.

## WHO DO YOU CLASH WITH?

As Dynamos value convention, they are usually at odds with those who seek out the new and disruptive. A Dynamo may find it draining to work with someone who prefers unstructured conversations and the abstract over details. As Dynamos are so committed, another a pet peeve of theirs is flakiness. Whether at work or in friendships, Dynamos are particularly irked by a *laissez-faire* attitude and someone who constantly reschedules. While Dynamos will be patient initially, their annoyance will build up over time. As a Dynamo, if you do find yourself working closely with such personality types, try to schedule a conversation early to discuss your different working styles and manage expectations.

## WHO DO YOU WORK WELL WITH?

Although they may clash initially, Dynamos can work happily with those who are more creative, abstract and driven by their emotions. When the relationship is managed well, a spontaneous and expressive approach is a good complement to a Dynamo's more structured one. Regardless of who they work with, Dynamos require clearly defined roles to meet their need for structure and certainty.

## WHO DO YOU HAVE A SECRET CRUSH ON?

As Dynamos are ordered and systematic in their thinking, they are likely to have a detailed checklist of what they are looking for in a partner. Unlike other personality types, Dynamos have a specific romantic type and are less open to deviating from that. On dating apps, Dynamos will rarely swipe right and are hesitant to be set up by friends unless they have enough information on their potential date. On a date, Dynamos will often be on a fact-finding mission rather than being fully present to the experience. As a Dynamo, if you try being a bit more flexible and open, you might be pleasantly surprised.

## WHO DO YOU WISH YOU WERE MORE LIKE?

As Dynamos are geared towards achievement, they are particularly inspired by stories of individuals who, through hard work and determination, forged their own path to success. Leaders of Fortune 500 companies and self-made CEOs who can juggle multiple pursuits and interests are likely role models. In work roles and social situations, introvert Dynamos may at times aspire to be more like those who are very comfortable asserting themselves in a large group setting such as a presentation and who communicate with ease. On the other hand, extravert Dynamos may value the listening skills of introvert Dynamos and their ability to take the pulse of social situations, picking up on social cues that others miss.

### A Dynamo's Playlist

'9 to 5', Dolly Parton

'*Clair de Lune*', Claude Debussy

'Make You Feel My Love', Adele

'Piano Man', Billy Joel

'My Girl', The Temptations

# In Friendships and Family

### DYNAMOS ARE RESPONSIBLE

A Dynamo's word is worth its weight in gold. Dynamos will rarely be late (in fact, they're usually a little early) or flake on social plans. Dynamos are used to making commitments and sticking to them and set themselves high standards for maintaining consistency and reliability. Dynamos may have similar expectations of timeliness and reliability of their friends and family, which can at times be unattainably high.

### DYNAMOS VALUE (PLANNED) QUALITY TIME

Dynamos enjoy spending time with family and friends, whether that's drinks after work or a Sunday picnic. However, Dynamos prefer to plan social activities in advance rather than be spontaneous, as they don't like to disrupt their weekly routine. While scheduling weeks in advance might be a turn-off for other personality types, Dynamos enjoy having things to look forward to and an excuse to get out their diary.

### DYNAMOS LIKE FAMILIAR HANGOUTS

Dynamos find comfort in the familiar – once they find something that works, they tend to stick to it. Dynamos are likely to have a favourite restaurant, café and fitness class, and are happy to rotate their chosen spots and activities rather than fill their calendar with every new pop-up or event that comes to town. The exception to this rule is travel, as Dynamos are happy to travel to new destinations, although they wouldn't say no to going back to a place filled with happy memories.

### DYNAMOS CRAVE STRUCTURE

Dynamos are drawn to routine and structure and, in friendships, tend to initiate a regular time to meet. In a family context, Dynamos have one of the most traditional parenting styles – they like a stable, nurturing and highly structured environment. Dynamo parents tend to be stricter than other parents, enforcing a daily routine. A family calendar is a staple on every Dynamo's kitchen fridge.

### DYNAMOS SEEK TRUST

Compared to other personality types, Dynamos prefer to have a close group of friends that they see regularly. Trust and loyalty, built over time, are an important foundation to a Dynamo's friendships and relationships, which is why they often prefer to see the same group of friends and have one-on-one catch-ups rather than more eclectic, spontaneous gatherings.

# In Romantic Relationships

### DYNAMOS VALUE DEPENDABILITY

Dependability is a priority on a Dynamo's relationship checklist. Dynamos approach their relationships, as most aspects of their life, from a rational perspective. They value partners who will meet both their short-term and long-term needs by being reliable and dependable. There's nothing that irks a Dynamo more than flakiness, especially in a relationship. Dynamos can be attracted to partners with different interests and backgrounds but an essential foundation is trust. This often makes Dynamos more attracted to partners with whom they can forge a longer-term relationship rather than have a short-term fling.

### DYNAMOS ARE ANALYTICAL

When weighing up an important decision in a relationship, Dynamos use rationality and logic rather than their 'gut instinct'. Although Dynamos recognise the importance of feelings and emotions, they don't let themselves be guided by them. Instead, Dynamos are naturally more analytical in their relationships, occasionally to the point of overthinking or over-analysing something a partner says or does, causing unnecessary stress and anxiety. For this reason, Dynamos are often suited to personality types that are more emotionally aware and can take Dynamos out of their over-analytical echo chamber from time to time.

### DYNAMOS VALUE HARMONY

Dynamos value a harmonious relationship and avoid conflict. They resist heated arguments or tense discussions as these can significantly deplete their energy. In a disagreement, Dynamos prefer to talk things through calmly, perhaps while walking through a park or catching up in a café. Dynamos will not be up for spending hours labouring over an argument and, to avoid this, they carefully weigh up another person's feelings before sharing their truth. This might help Dynamos avoid conflict but it can also mean that they fail to get what they need to off their chest. Dynamos should remember that they can be authentic and express what they feel while still being considerate towards others.

### DYNAMOS LIKE TO GIVE GIFTS

Dynamos are the planners in a romantic relationship. They are highly thoughtful gift-givers, often spending weeks looking for the perfect gift and the right card to accompany it. When it comes to planning romantic trips or activities, Dynamos are happy to take the reins, both because it gives them joy and because they like having that sense of control.

### DYNAMOS SEEK A SHARED VISION

Dynamos are happiest in relationships that have a stable, strong foundation from the start. Unlike other personality types, Dynamos are less likely to crave intense emotions and overwhelming lust and excitement. While Dynamos can be drawn to this initially, they prefer a steady building-up of feelings in a relationship. As Dynamos value goals and hard work, they aren't afraid to communicate their expectations of a partner and what they hope to give in return. Dynamos are comfortable putting effort into a relationship, as long as it's progressing towards a goal and a shared vision.

# Dynamos at Work

### DYNAMOS' DREAM JOB OR WORK ENVIRONMENT

Dynamos are typically drawn to professions that require analytical skills, clear goals and deadlines, such as consulting, engineering and data science. Dynamos thrive in positions that are structured, require attention to detail and are potentially more repetitive than other roles, as they respond best to clearly defined roles and guidelines. Dynamos do their best work in environments that are hierarchical, with transparent, clear authority.

## 5 Dream Jobs for a Dynamo

Data scientist    Project manager    Administrator    Doctor    Lawyer

## DYNAMOS ARE DRIVEN

Dynamos are goal-oriented and particularly driven to succeed. They have clear professional goals and are motivated to put in the hours and effort to achieve them. As Dynamos are highly conscientious, they may find themselves pushing themselves too hard at work while also striving for success in all other aspects of their life – friendships, relationships, hobbies and at home. As a Dynamo, be sure to set realistic expectations and be kind to yourself.

## PRACTICE MAKES PERFECT

Dynamos prefer to follow tested means to deliver to a consistently high standard, rather than push themselves and their team(s) out of their comfort zone to try new approaches for the sake of it. In leadership roles, Dynamos strive to create an environment in which colleagues have a clear understanding of their roles and responsibilities, and open channels of communication in case things go wrong. Dynamo leaders play a coordinating and managerial role and, while they are happy to offer emotional support, they are more suited to ensuring everyone shares the same vision and executes tasks to perfection. As a Dynamo, take care that your hard-working nature doesn't create unrealistic expectations of team members.

## DYNAMOS ARE LESS ADAPTIVE

As Dynamos do their best work within a clear framework, they may struggle to adjust to work scenarios that are uncertain or ambiguous. Situations that require a change in course or approach are likely to rattle a Dynamo's balance and sense of well-being. As a Dynamo, try not to panic when faced with an ambiguous problem as you may end up feeling paralysed. Staying calm is an important part of handling an unexpected situation.

## DYNAMOS ARE VALUED TEAM MEMBERS

Dynamos make dream team members: responsible, reliable and dependable – you can trust a Dynamo to keep their cool and help take a project to the finish line. When under pressure, Dynamos are happy to work tirelessly (even at the cost of their sleep) and will put in whatever effort is needed to get the work done to the highest standard. Dynamos can, however, be particular about doing things in a specific way and exacting about meeting a certain standard, and this can, at times, look like stubbornness, especially if faced with a suggestion of a different approach or a change in course. Challenges to their plan may ruffle a Dynamo's feathers and make them less receptive to feedback. As a Dynamo, try to cultivate a growth mindset: see challenges as opportunities and value the process, not just the end result.

# At Play

### DYNAMOS PERFECT A SKILL

Dynamos are classic achievers. Many Dynamos have a specific set of activities they enjoy, whether it be reading, cooking or a particular form of exercise. As a Dynamo who enjoys working towards a specific goal, set yourself micro-goals relating to a favourite activity. For example, if you love cooking, make a list of the three recipes you plan to master this month.

### DYNAMOS ORGANISE A TRIP

Dynamos love to plan and there's nothing more joyous to them than organising their next break, even if it's just a day trip to the seaside. Spend an afternoon researching activities, accommodation and things to see, then start building up the excitement for your next trip.

### DYNAMOS REORGANISE

Bringing order and cleanliness to their environment is a deeply ingrained habit for a Dynamo. As a Dynamo, lean in to this tendency and revel in making your space cosy and inviting. Keeping this goal in mind will make mundane chores enjoyable.

### DYNAMOS BUDGET CAUTIOUSLY

A Dynamo gets satisfaction, even joy, from budgeting, saving, spending wisely and never being late on a payment. As a Dynamo, try using a budgeting app to save towards splurge items and holidays.

### DYNAMOS RALLY THE COMMUNITY

Dynamos, especially extravert Dynamos, love to plan a get-together and to mobilise people for a good cause. As a Dynamo, flex your organisational skills and plan a fundraiser in your community.

## 5 Famous Dynamos

Sundar Pichai * Barack Obama * Hillary Clinton * Marie Curie * Oprah Winfrey

'Trying to do
it all and expecting
it all can be done
exactly right is a recipe
for disappointment.
Perfection is
the enemy.'

*

SHERYL SANDBERG

# Dynamos and Self-Care

### INDULGE YOUR INNER CHILD

As Dynamos are more analytic and pragmatic than other personality types, they can often get bogged down by work and the need to organise. Sometimes, indulging in artistic and creative activities, such as going to a pottery or painting class, can unleash tension and bring a new lease of life.

### DIGITAL DETOX

In our busy lives, we all need a digital detox every so often. Dynamos' drive and goal-orientation can mean that they hover close to their inbox much of the time. As a Dynamo, try to make a habit of switching off, even if it means putting your phone on airplane mode and in another room (or with a family member!) – do whatever works best for you.

### SPRING CLEAN

Embrace your inner Marie Kondo and spend an afternoon re-organising a category of belongings. Even if it's not spring, clean out your closet and re-organise your desk. You might like to colour code or invest in a label maker. Dynamos feel a sense of calm and control when things are neat and tidy – so take the time to indulge that habit.

### CHEAT DAY

A Dynamo is good at impulse control. Dynamos set and maintain long-range goals, they are deliberate in their choices and generally behave cautiously. Dynamos are particularly good at maintaining healthy eating habits and an active lifestyle. From time to time, though, plan to have a cheat day and indulge in something that is outside your typical routine – you deserve it.

### PRIORITISE A HEALTHY WORK-LIFE BALANCE

As Dynamos are hard-working and, often, perfectionists, they can sometimes forget to make time for themselves. Be sure to schedule time to unwind after a busy day of work: turn off phone notifications and do something that helps you to relax, whether that's cooking dinner, catching up with a friend, exercising or watching your favourite show.